EASY INSTRUCTOR
POLICE JIU-JITSU

EASY INSTUCTOR SERIES

POLICE JIU-JITSU

ALSO

VITAL HOLDS IN WRESTLING

FEATURING

KATO FUTSIAKA and PROF. BUTCH

*The Science of "Jiu-Jitsu" as Taught
to the Law Enforcement Bodies
in the United States and
Throughout the World*

Police, Marines "G" men, Soldiers, Sailors
And Members of the U.S. Coast Guard

FIFTY SIX ILLUSTRATIONS BY SEAMAN

The Naval & Military Press Ltd

Published by

The Naval & Military Press Ltd
Unit 5 Riverside, Brambleside
Bellbrook Industrial Estate
Uckfield, East Sussex
TN22 1QQ England

Tel: +44 (0)1825 749494

www.naval-military-press.com
www.nmarchive.com

*This book is published strictly for historical purposes.
The Naval & Military Press Ltd expressly bears no responsibility or
liability of any type, to any first, second or third party, for any
harm, injury, or loss whatsoever.*

*In reprinting in facsimile from the original, any imperfections are
inevitably reproduced and the quality may fall short of modern type
and cartographic standards.*

PART I

TABLE OF CONTENTS

Foreword	7
Points to Remember	9
Elementary Jiu-Jitsu	10
Simple Thumb Grip	12
Arm Lever and Fulcrum	13
Hammer Lock	15
Collar and Hip Throw	17
Falling Rock	20
The Cloture	22
Combination Finger, Hand and Leg	23
The Judicious Elbow	26
Disarming A Thug	28
Spread-Eagle	30
Swallowing the Apple	32
Each Man His Own Policeman	34
The Dervish	37
The Choke	38
The Ferris Wheel	42
Boxer's Descent	44
Lowered High Bridge	48
To Continue Our Feud with Boxers	52
In Which an Untutored Right Receives Instruction	55
Mill Race (or Pin Wheel)	56
Mill Race Modified	60
Breaking A Habit	63
The Push Over	64
Push Around	67
Turning Turtle	70
Mud Turtle	71
The Shears	73
Flying Prayer Wheel	75
Wherein We Discuss This and That	77

PART II

AMERICAN FORM OF WRESTLING

BODY SCISSORS	81
TOE AND ANKLE LEVER	84
COMBINATION ARM AND LEG TWINE AND BODY CHECK	85
THE STOCKS OR CHANCERY AND BODY CHECK	87
ARM PULL AND CROTCH LIFT	89
FLYING MARE	91
IN WHICH WE DISCUSS WRESTLING GENERALLY	92

FOREWORD

When Commander Perry opened up to the occidental world that shut-tight little island Kingdom, Japan, he did more than merely contact for our manufacturers a people who bought "Nifty Clothes," with two pair of pants. He gave us an insight into a world that was thoroughly organized and civilized long before Columbus discovered West where the East should have been.

The Japanese learned much from the so-called civilized world, but they taught us something we could never have learned from intercourse with any other nation. They gave our governmental forces of law and order a weapon that aided materially in the suppression of disorderly elements throughout our great cities. It took time, of course, to break down the prejudices that our early enforcement officers, in common with our then wild and wooly population, had against anything that was foreign. But when the great police forces of our largest metropolises realized that guns and billies alone would not be proof against big, burly lawbreakers, and that to instil respect in the hearts of "bruisers" they needed something other than armaments—pistols that could not be drawn fast enough,—they then discovered the wonder of Jiu-Jitsu.

They found that the wiley little brown man depended on brain instead of brawn and that he had developed a Science and an Art that utilized another's strength to his own undoing.

Strangely enough it was the layman who first appreciated the potential value of Jiu-Jitsu. For many years before the Police Forces of our cities put a study of this Science into the training of every rooky policeman, there were physical culture experts in America who advocated the use of it by everyone who had any respect for physical prowess but who found the spirit more willing than the flesh. They showed that it needed no possession of unusual strength to overcome an opponent that depended entirely on his bulk and ferocious appearnce to cow the meeker ones of the earth into submission.

The Japanese, by the very fact of their small stature, are compelled to place more emphasis on strategy than on force. Thus they have thoroughly developed Jiu-Jitsu and there is barely a saffron-hued tot in Japan that doesn't know something about the "Gentle-Art" as it is known.

President Masaryk of Czechoslovakia, one of the world's greatest educators, who, together with millions of his enlightened and progressive countrymen, is a firm believer in "a strong mind in a strong body," sought to teach every schoolboy in his country some knowledge of the wisest of all physical sciences.

While it does not itself develop and build muscle, it is an invaluable aid to the sensible use of the body. It is a form of wrestling that combines the cunning of the fox with the lithe grace and agility of the panther. It sharpens the brain and quickens the nerve centers.

The man or woman who has self-respect must not sit by and permit our people to become a nation of spectators watching athletic specialists perform, while we become obese and ungainly applauders. Jiu-Jitsu gives the man, woman and child, denied by nature a great frame, the opportunity to walk without fear, to resist successfully the bullies of their particular world, and the self-confidence which only a "well-armed" athlete can have. By its use, differences in weight, height and reach are practically wiped out, so that he who knows, may smilingly face superior odds and conquer.

POINTS TO REMEMBER

The devotee of Jiu-Jitsu need have no great knowledge of anatomy to locate for himself the few paralyzing centers of the human system. Very few pople are without the elementary fact that there is a region below the ears, where, if pressure is applied, an excruciating, shooting pain will ensue that will make the bully docile and easily subdued.

That at the juncture of the elbow and forearm there is a nerve center sometimes known as the "funny-bone," where, if scientifically manipulated, the student may actually disarm his opponent with ease.

That the shins are the tenderest part of the body and can withstand little if any pressure.

The postures shown in the diagram generously distributed throughout this volume will clearly indicate these vulnerable points of attack; and the holds which will place the student in the positions calculated to best effect the use of this common knowledge.

Remember that some of the tricks of Jiu-Jitsu may become dangerous to an inexperienced hand. It would be simple to permanently injure your helpful friend, if in your zeal, you put too much energy into a push or pull. Go easy.

With some application, the exercise of reasonable care and intelligence, you may become an expert at Jiu-Jitsu and experience the thrill that comes with the mastery of an Art that will imbue you with self-confidence, and by virtue of your ability to dominate others, if need be, impose a self-restraint that will win friends for you everywhere.

POLICE JIU-JITSU

ELEMENTARY JIU-JITSU

Assume that you are in a crowd; a particularly vicious person keeps pushing and shoving you. You protest and he becomes belligerent. The crowd soon enough makes room for you.

The other's reaction is to make a threatening move toward you.

Fig. 1

He throws his arm (usually his right, unless he is a professional "pug") forward.

Step forward, grasp his hand with your left. Press your four fingers firmly into the palm of the bully's hand, immediately beneath the thumb. Dig your thumb into the back of his hand; then bend his hand backward and jerk it downward.

If his resistance is greater, use both hands to bear down heavily on his wrist and arm.

Fig. 2

At the same time, as you step closer to him, interpose your left leg behind his right foot, making sure your heel is up against the inside of his right heel.

With the proper amount of pressure your opponent will either fall heavily to the ground, or find his wrist snap like a straw. (*See Fig. 1*)

Should your hasty friend be one who knows something of boxing and lead with his left, simply reverse the process. Grasp his left hand with your right, taking a stance something similar to that of a fencer, with your right foot forward, left back, left arm on hip. If he gives you more trouble than you anticipated, use both hands. (*See Fig.* 2)

Execute all this with a gentle, good humored smile—a nonchalance that will at once disguise your exertion and stamp you as a cool, collected person, dangerous to oppose.

SIMPLE THUMB GRIP

You are walking alone on a deserted street, secure in your honesty of purpose.

Fig. 3

You are accosted by a foot-pad, who sees your open countenance and simple smile. He moves his right arm to grasp you. His hand is open to seize some part of your body.

Again you fall into your fencing pose, standing directly in front of him, facing him. You shoot your right arm forward, with fingers outstretched.

Lock your hand around his, contriving to grasp his thumb by winding your four fingers around the back of his hand, your thumb inserting its way between the crotch formed by the division of his thumb and four fingers. (*See Fig. 3*)

By squeezing your four fingers firmly into the back of his hand, below the thumb, and bending his thumb back with yours, you will cause him to give ground. To avoid agonizing pain, the possible breaking of his thumb, he will be compelled to bend his knees. The continued pressure will result in his measuring his full length on the ground.

Thus, with not enough exertion to work up a healthy perspiration, you will have incapacitated a cowardly foot-pad, who will have too much respect for your prowess to follow you, when you calmly turn your back on him and walk smilingly away.

ARM LEVER AND FULCRUM

This is a tiny bit more complicated, but as usual, based on the simplest of scientific principles. Every public school boy knows how a lever and fulcrum works. Its application to the human body is one of the simple wonders of Jiu-Jitsu.

Imagine yourself honorary usher at a football game. An exceedingly noisy rowdy has been annoying some pretty co-ed. Chivalry, besides duty, demands that you squelch him. You have asked him repeatedly to stop. This is the last time and you march over to him determinedly.

He aims a swing at you with is right. You step back and a little to his right. With your right hand you seize his wrist. Draw his arm across your chest, in the general direction in which he threw it. Throw your left arm over his arm at his elbow, and completely encircling his arm, your left hand resting on your chest.

The wrist of your left arm urges a bony fulcrum into his forearm, while your right hand still holding his, constitutes a lever,

Fig. 4

with which he remains imprisoned in your grasp, unable to move.

Then by insinuating your right leg behind your opponent's right, your heel inside his, you cause him to be putty in your hands.

Kick your right foot against his and he will fall to the ground. You have won your point—squelched a rowdy and restored order. Imagine the reward from the blue eyes of that co-ed.

Oh yes, he would like to resist, but if he does, there's that pain of your right hand pressing on his arm, your left wrist gouging his forearm unmercifully and his arm in danger of breaking. Here's how it looks: (*See Fig.* 4)

HAMMER LOCK

You are celebrating the victory of your college team, no small portion of your enjoyment being the fact that you helped to win, and "the" best girl is hanging on your arm, gazing soulfully into her hero's eyes. You are stepping out of a cab, about to enter a restaurant, when a member of the day's opposing team—or maybe it's a disgruntled fan—who undoubtedly lost a dime or two betting against you, makes a disparaging remark.

Fig. 5

16   POLICE JIU-JITSU

You pay no attention. You cannot become embroiled in rough-house when she's with you. The other takes it for cowardice. He sidles up with blood in his eye. You cannot disregard that. You gently disengage your fair companion's arm.

The slightly squiffy fan let's go his right in your general di-

Fig. 6

rection. Perfectly calm, but with the steel of resolution, you side step and duck a shade to the right; grab his wrist with your left hand, raising it aloft. Quickly you run under his arm, holding onto his wrist all the while, and then wheel around to the left. Twist his arm around and step with it in back of the almost shell-shocked opponent, pressing his twisted arm against his own back. He will make little effort to resist, because you are twisting his arm with restrained but determined fierceness.

If he does struggle too much, since you are then standing directly behind him, and your right arm is free, just snap your right arm over his right shoulder, bend your hand forward tucking it under his chin, and with a right and back pressure, pull his head backward.

In less time than it takes him to recover his sense, he is as much your prisoner as if you had handcuffed his hands and locked his neck in a vise. (*See Fig. 5*)

Of course no gentleman, in the presence of his lady fair would dream of doing anything further about subduing this unthinking pest, except of course in that same quiet manner demanding an apology from the very-much humbled fan. He will be a very much sadder but wiser man, if he doesn't readily accede to your quiet request.

You have maintained your calm, your poise, and you can rest assured have lost nothing in the esteem of your lovely lady. (*See Fig. 6*)

COLLAR AND HIP THROW

A gentle answer, they tell us, turneth away wrath. And there are those who say, if attacked, turn the other cheek. There are times, however, when silence is gold, and the best thing to turn is the other man.

You are seeing your best friend off on the ornate ocean liner and are about to board the ship for a last glimpse of her beloved face. A singularly vicious, and slightly inebriated sailor, foreign to your land and to your gentlemanly instincts, dislikes your face. He couldn't tell why. But he doesn't. He feels an irresistible impulse to change the contour of your face, and first shouts some obscene oaths. Failing to disturb you, he aims what he thinks is a perfect hay-maker for your eye.

You would be properly ornamented the next day if you did not know Jiu-Jitsu. But you do.

You duck his swing, or fade or side-step to the left. Encountering no solid body, our sailor will necessarily have his body at an unprotected angle and slightly bent forward. His arm, too, will have lowered.

Fig. 7

Being immediately to his left and behind his arm, you raise your right arm, push his away, slide your arm over his, reaching all the way across to his left shoulder, where you will seize his coat collar. Your arm by then will be directly resting on his throat. Your body will be so placed that your left hip will rest against his, and if you know your holds, you will then place your left foot

POLICE JIU-JITSU 19

directly behind both of his, bend your own body forward, and whether he will or no, he will have to follow your body backwards, your arm under his throat strangling him, until he is more than willing to cry "uncle". Or anyway—cry. Or try to pick himself off the ground. (*See Fig. 7*)

Having mastered this seemingly intricate throw, although actually it is one of the simplest of all the Jiu-Jitsu tricks, the student

Fig. 8

is definitely launched on the sea that leads to complete knowledge and enjoyment of the Art. From there, while almost infinite in their variety, Jiu-Jitsu holds and postures are but variations and improvements on this simple theme. (*See Fig. 8*)

POLICE JIU-JITSU

FALLING ROCK

You are a quiet person. You have been taught that the meek inherit the earth. You have been meek all your life and have inherited practically nothing else. But you have latent power—you have a certain knowledge given to few people in occidental countries. You know something about Jiu-Jitsu.

Fig. 9

But there are others who are possessed of more. They are possessed of bulk and mean dispositions. One of these chip-on-shoulder inheritors has singled you out for his peculiar brand of humor. You seem so small and defenseless.

You are impervious to his remarks and he becomes peevish. His muscles are more active than his brain. Before he knows it he craves action, and directs a right handed blow at you.

Still unperturbed—meekly—you duck. You have been standing facing him. You turn to the left and as he moves his right arm forward you catch his wrist with your left hand. You do not stop the action there.

Using his own force—you pull his arm further forward over your left shoulder; you bend under his arm—stoop—grip the back of his left leg with your right hand, just in back of his knee: (*See Fig. 9*)

Suddenly you straighten up and with the same motion, con-

Fig. 10

tinue to pull on his outstretched arm, but now downward. Your action is so fast that your opponent's own off-balance punch, has helped you pull him in the same direction he was going.

By straightening up, your right shoulder pressing into his midriff, your left arm pulling his right arm, all you have to do is to bend your own body lower and he flies over your left shoulder—

22 POLICE JIU-JITSU

over and beyond your head, landing on his own, some distance away. (*See Fig.* 10)

You can afford a modest smile. With unruffled dignity, you can stand and watch your bulky opponent, the chip now off his shoulder, his spirit chastened, pick himself up. He is a bit bewildered. His rise was sudden but his fall was meteoric. He doesn't know it, but you have given him a lesson in "dumping the load". You have taught him to respect what the Japanese call "Shoinage", or perhaps we might coin a phrase in our own expressive language and name it the "Falling Rock."

THE CLOTURE

It is a peculiarity of most men who resort to fists, before thought, that they think, if at all, of "aiming" a blow. Their action is automatic, and they let fly with the muscle most under

Fig. 11

control, i.e., that limb which is most co-ordinated with the brain. Thus most people "aim" a right.

All else having failed, you now have no time to reason with such a person. When he attempts to strike, you must put him "hors de combat" or find your dignity, together with your body, in a reclining position.

Then what?

Simply duck under that "right" and come closer to him, facing him in such a way that his right arm passes over your left shoulder.

Then step your left foot forward; place it right in back of his right foot, your heel touching his.

Lift your right hand up till the heel of your palm touches his chin. Press forward with force, and his head will snap backward.

Then with your free left hand, fist doubled, you hit him in the small of his back, forcing his body to bend further back.

Here too, your leg acts as a fulcrum. Your hand on his chin as a lever. If this action is rapid and well-coordinated, you will have practically no difficulty in throwing him heavily backward to land on some part of his anatomy and in a spot he hasn't chosen. You will put a "cloture" on his physical ambitions. (*See Fig.* 11)

Perhaps the simplest of all Jiu-Jitsu throws, and the most unexpected, the "cloture" is more thoroughly effective than the use of a heavy and dangerous weapon. You put the quietus on an obnoxious individual who will think twice before again picking on a harmless looking prospect. He will learn that discretion pays dividends where valor might be a complete loss.

COMBINATION FINGER, HAND AND LEG

If the friend who has so kindly consented to act as your guinea pig for the experiments we have suggested still feels up to this gentle mayhem, you might further impose on him to have him impersonate a bully again and show him another simple Jiu-Jitsu trick.

For want of a real translation of the Japanese idiom, let's, for all practical purposes, call it the "simple finger bend, hand push and leg throw". That omits no essential part of the action.

To dramatize the situation, let him assume a rage he doesn't feel; let him pretend you have taken his best girl and you have words over that fact. If he is sufficiently realistic, he will try to

Fig. 12

punch you, or to seize you around the body to inflict punishment on you. He will extend his left arm, let us say.

To further carry on the drama, you will then grab his hand with your right, so that your thumb presses into the back of his hand. Your fingers will bore into his palm.

Having secured that hold, you will bend his hand backward, towards him, but first having placed yourself to his left, so that the pressure of his hand backward will be toward his body, but somewhat at right angles thereto: (*See Fig.* 12)

Meanwhile you will assume the fencing pose, but this time you will place your left foot behind his left foot, your heel touching his, your knee slightly bent.

Fig. 13

If your presure on his hand, and the twist you are using on his arm and hand do not throw him backward, you can then bring up the heel of the palm of your left hand, which you will note is free, and place it against his chin. Then you will push his head back, until perforce he will be compelled to give ground, when your interposed leg will trip him so that he will have to fall. (*See Fig.* 13)

I trust this unhappy experience will not discourage your worthy friend from helping you further. If he cavils at always being your victim, be a good fellow and let him try it on you. It will be a salutary and instructive lesson to both.

THE JUDICIOUS ELBOW

Somehow you managed to become ensnarled in this Mardi-Gras crowd. The spirit of the occasion is entirely genial. Everybody is laughing—or should be. But one big, burly fellow with the air of a misanthrope, an acid expression on his moon-face, is elbowing all the revelers to the right and left of him. This "bear

Fig. 14

that walks like a man" has had the milk of human kindness dried up in him. His indiscriminate shoving and mauling has awakened the protector in you.

POLICE JIU-JITSU

Nevertheless you are unwilling to depart from your habitual calm. Suddenly you see him pushing a little wisp of a miss from his path. She seems so fragile and helpless that the big brother in you rebels.

You walk over to him and ask him in what you believe to be a gentlemanly manner, why he doesn't behave. His sneer at your own effrontery is a masterpiece. You are not much larger than

Fig. 15

the diminutive girl, and he thinks he can break you in two.

He puts both ham-like paws on your shoulders, then slips his arms around you. Truly like some bear meaning to crush you.

You yield so prettily that he is deceived.

Just as he is about to exert some more pressure, you bring your right elbow up until the sharp point of it jams into his Adam's Apple. He will begin to gag almost at once.

Then you move your left foot behind his right, resting your

heel against his; you form the fingers of your left hand into a rigid hook and with them you rap sharply against the small of his back. And then keep pressing at that point.

Exerting extraordinary pressure of your elbow against his throat, you throw him over your left leg, so that he falls backwards. (*See Fig.* 14)

Should your sour-faced opponent be just a bit more difficult to subdue with the hooked fingers in his back, you can easily vary the action, so that you grasp his right arm at a point just a bit below his elbow, twisting it downward, and at the same time pressing your right elbow into his Adam's Apple.

With these combined pressures you can easily throw him over.

Of course, it is the "judicious elbow" that has actually incapacitated him from active resistance. The excruciating pain caused by the contact of your elbow with his throat will make him unwilling to keep up the feud. If this doesn't sober up his viewpoint and make him look on his fellow man with more tolerance, at least it will remove a dangerous, disruptive element from the joy of the festive occasion. (*See Fig.* 15)

DISARMING A THUG

Thus far we have discussed the ordinary contingencies of life— the attack by and the conquest of those who rely on their superior physical attainments.

It may well be argued that we have not, till now, considered the greater menace to peace and contentment, the armed thug. Is he, too, amenable to the persuasive quality of Jiu-Jitsu? Our answer, of course, is YES.

Let's consider the man with a weapon.

Unless he be one of those hardened criminals we have become familiar with during Prohibition, the gun-toting thug, he does not ordinarily carry his weapon in a shoulder holster. He keeps it for occasional use, in his back or hip-pocket.

Its possession strengthens his cowardly courage and he is always fully aware of its position. To make sure, he usually pats it slyly, particularly when its use becomes imminent.

Watch him out of the corner of your eye. Then quietly sidle up to him. Being always on the defensive, he will make a dive for his hip. His elbow forms a loop with the insertion of his hand into his back-pocket.

NOW YOU HAVE THE PROPER OPENING.

If it be his right hand—and it usually is—you step immediately to his left.

Fig. 16

With the speed of light, you must spring to the attack.

You slip your left arm into the loop he has unconsciously formed. Continue sliding your arm around until it reaches his left shoulder.

You then bring your free, right arm up in front of him and across the same shoulder until both your arms meet—hand to hand.

You have now formed a compelling vise. The arm you have

slipped through the loop of his arm keeps forcing his shoulder down, while at the same time, it obliges his elbow to rise with your arm. Your right arm across the front of his shoulder is doing heroic service. It is pressing that overworked shoulder downward too. Before he knows it, he is beginning to resemble a jackknife.

To complete his downfall, you place your right foot directly in front of his, and with an extra jerk of both your arms on his poor, burdened shoulder, he would have to possess superhuman strength to save himself from being thrown to the ground. (*See Fig.* 16)

It then becomes a simple matter to extract from his hip-pocket the weapon you feared, but which has now become as impotent as a rattle snake without its poisonous sac. When and if your lowbrow friend recovers his composure and some measure of the use of his feet, he will undoubtedly give you as wide a berth as he can.

So with guile you have subdued guilt.

SPREAD-EAGLE

Pride, it is said, goeth before a fall. And, we may add, pride of brute force used promiscuously, deserveth a fall.

However, to purge such pride, it isn't always necessary to take a fall out of it. In jiu-jitsu, by the use of the Spread-Eagle, it is possible to hurt so severely, that the cry of "Lay on MacDuff" will quickly change to "Enough."

Let's suppose the party's "prize pest" is at it again. He feels, as he always does when friends foregather, like torturing you, who are smaller. He has done it so often, he thinks he will have another field day at your expense.

His arms hang down in that swinging fashion he assumes when about to commence his usual banter of tapping you with light, taunting jabs on the nose. You have always taken it, hoping he would wear himself out soon. How can he now believe that you would resent it? Or that you know how to stop it?

POLICE JIU-JITSU

You close in on him, pretending to shorten the distance so that his blows might become ineffective.

Deftly you seize his left hand with your right. Part of your palm covers the back of his hand; your thumb touches his little finger; the other four fingers fitting into the crotch between his thumb and fingers; your finger-tips gripping their way into the palm of his hand, thus: (See Fig. 17)

Fig. 17

You hold tightly on to his hand. Then step to his left and swing with his hand, completely in back of him. You bend your own elbow upward. This will force his elbow up; the point of your elbow will fit into the crook of his.

Then, having him firmly in your power, you twist his hand outward, with a circular motion, while holding his elbow rigid.

This will cause shooting pains to sweep through his arm and wrist.

Now, don't be so naive as to think he will yield quietly. Oh, no. Remember his right arm is still free. He cannot turn his body, but he can swing his arm. He does—across his chest, hoping to strike your face which is in back of his head.

However, you haven't forgotten the balance of this lesson. Quickly you follow up with your free, left arm. You reach across his left shoulder; place your left hand against the left side of his face.

You push, with force. His head will snap to the right, while his left hand is being twisted unmercifully to the left.

He is spread-eagled.

All he can do, if at all, is to impotently thresh his right hand across his chest with that useless motion.

Soon, too soon, he must be convinced that he must ask for mercy or have his wrist snapped like a pipe-stem and his neck have a crick in it for a long time to come.

To paraphrase, with apologies, that delightful poem of Sir Walter Scott, in this connection:
>Lives there a man with soul so dead,
>Who will not, by then, to himself have said:
>I'd better cry quits—or lose hand and head,
>I'll change my ways and go off to bed.

SWALLOWING THE APPLE

When Adam took that fateful apple from Eve some few years back, he started something. From the behavior of some men in the crowded subways of our modern cities, you would think the latter day Adam is trying to take his downfall out on poor Eve's descendants. He crowds, shoves and pushes her sisters with a vim and a venom no serpent of Eden would have dreamed of.

Our Eve should learn a trick or two to purge the pushing and shoving Adam of his intentional or unconscious roughness toward her. She should give him the "Swallowing the Apple" again. It will be all the more effective because it is so unexpected.

Here's how it's done.

She grabs him by the sleeve of his jacket with her right hand, allowing his arm to fall under her bent elbow, like this: (*See Fig. 18*)

While still maintaining her ladylike composure, she will step forward, so that her right foot is directly behind his left leg, while she herself stands firmly grounded on her own left leg in back of her.

Fig. 18

With the fingers of her left hand, held stiffly together, she will jab her hand into his Adam's Apple. This will snap his head back and cause a constriction in his throat, that will teach him good manners in the most graphic way. He will soon feel as though he is "swallowing the Apple."

He would like to retreat, but her right foot is behind his left leg and he cannot move his body without falling.

He'll take it—and will not like it.

Our male student need not turn up his nose at this simple Jiu-Jitsu trick merely because we have indicated that it may be done by his long suffering sister.

Certainly we do not recommend his using this drastic though easy remedy against the sometimes just as flagrant female offender. We cannot—and retain our reputation for chivalry. It's the badge of our male affliction. This we must suffer silently.

But one needn't pamper the manly subway-hog, who, constantly treads on your toes, breathes what his "best friends won't tell him" into your face and rests his avoirdupois on your unwilling body.

A light, gentlemanly jab with the stiffened fingers in his Adam's Apple, in the manner suggested above, will instil painful respect and future thoughtfulness. You may even reform him—if that be possible.

EACH MAN HIS OWN POLICEMAN

It's Saturday. Before Christmas.

You have just withdrawn the money you have saved by doing without three cigars and one soda per week, from your bank's Christmas Club.

You're going to get that wrist-watch Nellie's been talking about. You want to see that starry-eyed wonder in her eyes when you present her with it.

You are gazing into the jeweller's window, wondering whether the sign reads $85.00 or $35.00; the price-tag seems slightly blurred. Or maybe you've been looking at it too long!

You feel a gentle tug at your coat pocket. You are startled! You have the envelope with the money there. Someone is trying to obtain Christmas cheer with your money!

You pretend to be unaware of that light-fingered gent's hand

POLICE JIU-JITSU 35

as it blissfully withdraws the envelope from your pocket. You have studied Jiu-Jitsu.

Suddenly you seize that withdrawing hand with both of yours.

You press both thumbs into the back of that stealthy hand. Your fingers bore into the pick-pocket's palm. You hold it imprisoned as in a vise.

Fig. 19

You wheel around rapidly with that captive hand still clutched in yours. Speed is your only salvation. He's a big, burly fellow.

You twist his hand upward and back. By then he has dropped your envelope.

You keep pressing his hand back, raising his arm on high. You

POLICE JIU-JITSU

now have him where you may even release one of your hands and with it press the small of his back, so he will be forced to his knees. (*See Fig.* 19)

You can hold him thus, until one of the regular guardians of the law arrive. The police will take care of his future. But until then, you have demonstrated that each man may be his own policeman.

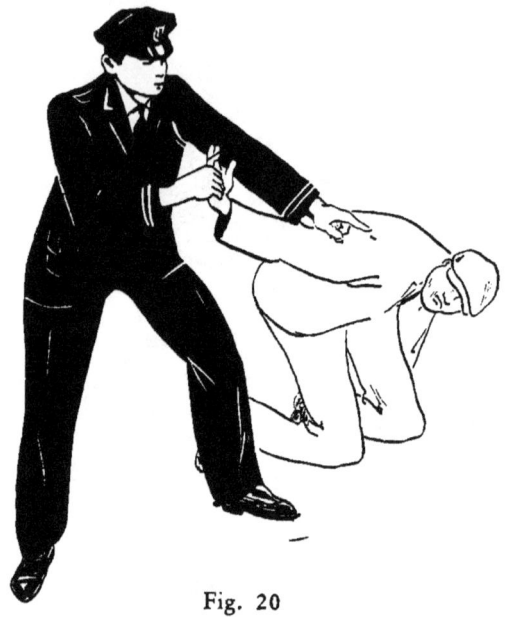

Fig. 20

And you have also proved to everyone's satisfaction that Nellie's man may be incurably romantic on Christmas, but he is still sufficiently the man to safeguard his loved one's Yuletide treasure.

With renewed vigor you can go into the jeweller's, and with a firmer voice ask to see the $35.00 wrist-watch. (*See Fig.* 20)

THE DERVISH

The Arabs have a sect of holy men known as Dervishes. For some reason known best to themselves, they pray best when they whirl like some animated windmill.

While not discounting the efficacy of prayer, the Jiu-Jitsu artist need have no recourse to divine assistance to do his stint. He must, however, emulate the Arab holy man if he desires to execute the "Dervish" and must whirl with the same kaleidoscopic rapidity.

Fig. 21

Suppose Public Enemy No. 16, has just held you up at the point of a gun; taken your wallet with all your ten singles in it, and is stalking away, his back turned to you with the contempt criminals have for cowed citizens.

Now is your chance (if you have recovered your senses).

You take one or two soft steps toward him.

Steal your right arm over his right shoulder, across his neck, around it; and grasp the collar of his coat on the left side, holding firmly. Ball your left hand into a hard fist and slam it into his left buttock. This will force his body forward and his head backward. The bony part of your right wrist jams it's way into his Adam's Apple.

This is just the beginning of the action.

You then drop to your left knee, bending your right leg to form a stumbling block. You continue. Vigorously you press the right arm and wrist across his throat and pull him backward. He falls over the right knee you have just prepared for him.

Normally he would fall on his back. But you have prepared a worse fate for him.

As he falls he naturally stretches out his arms to balance himself.

You seize his left arm with your left hand and bend it in such a way that his body is turned over—onto his face.

You then disengage your right arm from under his throat, but only far enough to grasp his chin and twist it upward and away from the ground.

To keep him passive in this punishing position, you lower your right knee to press into the small of his back. While further to imprison him, you grasp his right arm with your right and stretch it upward. (*See Fig.* 21)

This is the most devastating and utterly demoralizing hold imaginable. If you study it carefully and learn to co-ordinate all the movements with speed and precision, you will most likely, by means of this one trick alone, justify all the energy and effort you have given to Jiu-Jitsu. It will establish you at once as an athlete of no mean parts. You will be the terror of your enemies and the joy of your friends.

THE CHOKE

There is probably no single police force in the world whose members have not received instruction in some form of Jiu-Jitsu. The universal recognition of this science has undoubtedly revolutionized the art of apprehending malefactors without the aid of firearms.

In the United States, where every citizen is required, if need be, to render aid and assistance to the duly constituted authorities, a knowledge of the "CHOKE" may prove invaluable.

A story is told which illustrates best the wholesome effect of even a primary familiarity with Jiu-Jitsu. In this case, the use of the "choke" by a young bank clerk averted a terrible catastrophe. It had a happy ending, otherwise we would be loath to tell it.

Fig. 22

B. was a wealthy banker; quite philanthropic, public spirited, and more or less famous for these benefactions. During the last market debacle, however, he, together with his business brethren fell very much in disrepute. The papers were daily berating some banker for criminal speculation and the consequent destruction of depositors' money.

On this day, the story goes on to tell, B. was in his inner

sanctum, when the door opened silently. Some sixth sense caused B. to look up. He saw before him a well-dressed young man, who had a strange glitter in his eyes.

Needless to say B. was startled. He couldn't imagine how this young man had gotten into his office without being announced. He so stated to his visitor.

"B.," the young man half-whispered. "I have here in my hand (he was holding a square package) enough nitro-glycerine to blow this whole building to hell-an-gone. I should do so, because your class has wiped out the savings of the poor. But that would

Fig. 23

rid the world of only one parasite without doing me any good. Listen carefully.

"I want $20,000. in cash—at once. I am asking for this small sum only, because I believe it is the easiest to obtain without any great flurry of excitement.

"Ring for your manager. Talk casually. Don't raise your

voice too loudly. Don't by word or movement betray the situation, or you will accompany me to a place where neither your relatives or mine will ever be able to find us. Ask him to get you $20,000. in small denominations."

There was no mistaking the youth's words or his mien. It was quiet but desperate.

B. could not but acquiesce. He felt responsible for the lives not only of his own person and employees, but of every other human in the biulding.

He rang the bell. Young G. responded to the call.

G. was a member of the Y. M. C. A., an athlete, and a youngster of discernment. Somehow, no one yet knows why or how, he sensed a strained atmosphere. Perhaps it was the tremor in his employer's voice, or some vague premonition.

He saw a square package resting at the feet of the visitor. The latter had placed it there to avoid the appearance of the unusual and because he wanted to be able to kick it if it became necessary.

G. turned to leave the room, but out of the corner of his eye he noted the nervous motions of the visitor.

He whirled on his heel. Glided up behind the visitor. He reached his right arm across the latter's shoulder (right shoulder), grasped his coat lapel on the left side, digging his bony wrist into the desperado's throat.

His right foot he placed on the back rung of the chair in which the visitor sat. He tilted the chair backward.

To save himself from falling, the man stretched out his left arm. G. seized his left wrist with his right hand and swung it toward himself. The rapid action threw the man backward; the jerk on his arm forced him to fall off the side of the chair and flat on to his face, the chair sliding away from his to the side and against the desk.

With the man safely on the floor, and fortunately a distance away from the package which lay undisturbed, G. placed his right knee on the man's shoulder, pinning him to the ground, and forced his left arm upward.

Then for the first time he withdrew the choking right arm and wrist from around his throat, but did not let up entirely. He grasped his chin, forcing his head upward from the floor.

The action, except for the fact of the man having been seated, was very much like the "Dervish" described in a previous chapter. It was, however the "CHOKE" that held the man powerless and as putty in the hands of the young athlete. But for that punishing, hold, the criminal might have been able to wriggle out of the toils and accomplished destruction. We give you a picture of how it looked to the astonished B. who watched the action in paralyzed wonder. (See Fig. 22)

Suffice it to say that young G. was thereafter regarded with more than passing admiration and respect. He had saved the life of an important person, aside from the many whose careers he had salvaged.

The box, upon being opened, disclosed a dreadful amount of explosive. The man had not been lying.

It is given to very few of us to act so promptly in an emergency. That, of course, amounts almost to genius. But young G. attributes his present success entirely to his knowledge of Jiu-Jitsu. He had been for some time the butt of all the other employees' jokes for his application to this form of physical exercise. He is now, and will always be, the envy of those who sneered. (See Fig. 23)

THE FERRIS WHEEL

Most modern gymnasiums devoted to the patrons of pugilism also cater to the Murderers of the Mat. A certain amount of petty persiflage between the cults occurs at intervals. The fighters, no less cauliflowered than the wrestlers, enjoying the greater esteem of the public, have an edge in the argument. They claim with vehemence and a vast willingness to demonstrate, that the poorest boxer is a match for the best wrestler.

Whatever may be the merits of both schools of "learning," we, who haunt the sacred preserves of the "pugs" and the "pachy-

POLICE JIU-JITSU 43

derms" for thrills, chills and laughs, have, of course, a pet theory of our own. Haven't we all?

To prove our own thesis, we inveigled little Kato Futsiaka, (an honest Japanese school-boy from Columbia) into accompanying us to Prof. Butch's Academy of Annihilation (for the best of reasons, that is not the name of the place).

There after various and sundry bragging and boasting, we induced a rather blatantly belligerent battler to test his skill in boxing against Kato's knowledge of Jiu-Jitsu. If one American

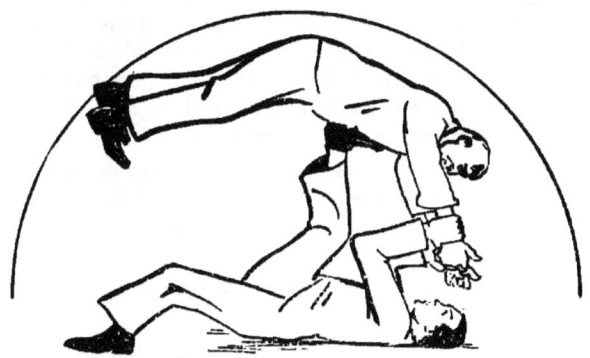

Fig. 24

is better than five "furriners" (and who dreams that is otherwise?), poor little Kato should receive a lethal blow in short order and his remains, if any, would have to be claimed by the Japanese Navy (if it could find them).

Battling Beauty squared off and with a lowering leer faced nimble footed Kato.

B.B. let fly a left which should have squashed K. like a fly under a swatter.

K. didn't move out of the way. He grasped the fighter's wrist with steel like fingers. B.B. followed up with a right, which he had held in reserve.

Kato grasped the right wrist of his opponent.

Swift as light, he put up his right leg until it rested in the pit of B.B.'s stomach.

The force of the fighter's blows was such, that, together with the pull which Kato exerted on the other's wrists, threw Kato backward and the fighter forward so that the little Jap fell to the ground, which luckily was covered by a mat. The behemoth would have been on top of him and probably crushed Kato, if it hadn't been for that obnoxious foot of his.

Feeling a solid floor beneath him, Kato lifted his foot higher, jerked the wrists of our boxer with more urgency and the bewildered "pug" found himself hoisted into the air and flying with the greatest of ease over and beyond the diminutive body—far to the rear of the mat, landing with a thud that threatened to shake the ancient timbers of the gymnasium.

Certainly the contest was over. B.B. was unconscious for some time, and everyone wondered how that could be, because most of the onlookers thought his head more solid than the concrete floor on which he had fallen.

How did Kato do it? Let's show you with a picture: (*See Fig. 24*)

Well, Kato told us the name of that trick. It had such an outlandish sound that we determined to call it the "Ferris Wheel" in our own mellifluous New Yorkese. At any rate it is a more descriptive name, if you know what we mean. B.B. rose high in the air, had his ride and came down. Unfortunately for him, he paid more and saw less. The scenic wonders, when he landed on his head, may have been nil but he did get a good view of many planetary bodies.

BOXER'S DESCENT

One product of our American civilization, proclaimed alike in song and story, is the fight promoter. He's usually a city dweller, and yet, in his way, a farmer of sorts. He, it is, who raises periodic crops of cauliflowers.

He has made the public fight conscious. So much so, that

POLICE JIU-JITSU 45

wherever sports foregather, there can be heard the classic, "He's got a good left," etc.

So men who box or fight, develop a "good left" and in fighting, lead with their lefts.

It is this tendency that gives the Jiu-Jitsu artist the great ad-

Fig. 25

vantage when he meets and faces the boxer.

Let's call in our little friend, Kato Futsiaka again. He's not the best of the exponents of our art, but he knows a good deal about it, and he's an enthusiast and articulate enough to explain it.

46 POLICE JIU-JITSU

Then having him with us, let's get a boxer in. A good one. Let's tell them to mix it.

The boxer, being orthodox, doesn't wait for his opponent to come to him. He rushes Kato and leads with his left.

Kato, the calm little artist, bends at the knees, ducking that pulverizing left and steps to the boxer's left and immediately to his rear.

Fig. 26

With his open palm he shoves B's left arm forward, steps directly in back of him, placing his left leg in between the spread legs of the fighter. The little Japanese bends his left knee, while keeping his right leg rigid and firmly on the ground in back of him.

He then snakes his left arm over the boxer's left shoulder,

POLICE JIU-JITSU 47

worms across his chest until he grasps the fighter's jacket collar on the right side, thus bringing his wrist against the latter's windpipe. (See Fig. 25)

Thereupon he proceeds to give the boxer a lesson in rapid motion.

He jabs a balled fist into the base of the fighter's spine, and pushes with vigor. This serves a two-fold purpose. It tends to

Fig. 27

inflict injury in a spot on the human anatomy that is particularly vulnerable, and it causes the boxer's body to move forward involuntarily to escape this punishment.

With his left arm, Kato pulls the other's head backward. He must go that way or have his wind shut off by that infernal pressure on his windpipe. (See Fig. 26)

The bent left leg of Kato now does its duty. The boxer's body comes in contact with it and he stumbles. He describes a backward arc, and the pressure of Kato's left arm twists his body to one side, so that when he falls, it will be on his right side.

Kato will then seize his left arm, hold it taut, while he sinks his right knee into the other's left shoulder where it meets his chest, keeping him in durance until the little wrestler decides to let go.

If the boxer shows signs of revitalization and wishes to dispute the fact of his lowered status, Kato need only bend forward and grasp his chin with one free hand, twisting it in whichever direction will give the prone boxer the most pain. (*See Fig.* 27)

Assuredly this is savage treatment for the boxing cock-of-the-walk, but then is there anything particularly civilizing or uplifting in a fist to the nose, even if it be encased in a boxing glove?

And it is interesting to note that the Jiu-Jitsu holds and falls may be actually accomplished without bloodshed. Except to the eyes of the sadistic spectator, the spectacle of a modern prizefight, especially between the "big boys" must be a horrifyingly gory adventure.

By contrast, Jiu-Jitsu is truly the "gentle art."

LOWERED HIGH BRIDGE

In these days of industrial warfare, labor and capital may be having it out over a principle, but usually any real injury occasioned is suffered by the innocent bystander.

A red-blooded American would rather remain innocent of interference, and prefers often not to be a bystander, but objects most strenuously to being injured.

If in the heat of labor conflict, you are stranded somewhere between opposing factions, and find yourself attacked by some ruffian with a stick or club, be he striker, strike-breaker, or just plain ruffian, you must defend yourself.

The rough will raise his stick to strike a blow at your head. If you duck, you may lessen the force of the blow, but receive it you will.

Again to your rescue comes your knowledge of Jiu-Jitsu, with its utilizing of the other's force and turning it into a weakness.

Instead of stepping away or dodging, which would be the normal impulse, you will step forward.

As his arm is raised on high, you will take your fencing stance,

Fig. 28

stepping forward with your right foot and raise your own arm. You would then ordinarily receive a paralyzing blow on the arm, if it were your intention to seize the stick. But your specialized knowledge tells you to grab his descending wrist and with it step to his right side, snapping his wrist away from his body so that what would be his palm faces you.

Then step still closer. Quickly place your left foot in front of his right foot on which he had been resting heavily because of his forward thrust with his stick or club.

Jerking his extended arm forward and in the same direction in which he had been going when he aimed his blow with the club, you find him bending forward.

Fig. 29

Your left leg hits up against the shin-bone of his right leg striking that prop right out from under him. He commences to fall forward. Nothing loath, you urge him on by pushing your left arm, which has been free from the start, against his bending shoulder. (*See Fig.* 28)

The whole movement, complicated as it may seem in the description thereof, takes place almost in the twinkling of an eye.

Executed with that celerity, he must fall face forward to the ground.

Once there, you sink to the ground on your knees, right near him, and with your left knee you dig into that extended right arm which is now stretched out on the ground. You haven't let go of his wrist, so that now you are clasping the wrist and pressing down on that same arm. (*See Fig. 29*)

Fig. 30

He is actually a prisoner, as if you had handcuffs on his hands. Should he show signs of failing to capitulate, you need now only bend over and place your left hand under his fallen chin and with little tenderness pull that chin upward, so that he is in the position of a Texas longhorn being hazed and "punched" by a cow-boy.

To all intents and purposes, all thoughts of combat will have completely left your fallen hoodlum. Thereafter, if he feels the urge to destruction again, he will most likely seek to strike other of his fellow combatants who have as little science as he, and leave the innocent bystander alone. He will long remember, though little note, that he has been given the "lowered high-bridge" for the good of his soul. (*See Fig. 30*)

TO CONTINUE OUR FEUD WITH BOXERS

Ferocity is often a deciding factor in what is sometimes called euphoniously, a "boxing contest."

It is no mere accident that finds a fighter in the ring with a week's wiry stubble on his rocky chin, looking for all the world, with his flattened nose and flapping ears, like some vicious orang-outang out of the jungle. This appearance is designed to frighten the life out of his opponent. And it would—if his partner in

Fig. 31

crime didn't present an apparition quite as, if not more frightful than he.

These Frankenstein monsters, however, often go into a song-and-dance that belies their seemingly vicious propensities, as attested by the varied loud boos and "Bronx" cheers of the really blood-thirsty customers.

Such an exhibition of ferocity, however, would not phase the "gentle artist."

If Beetle-brow, glowering pugnaciously were to let fly a lethal

Fig. 32

"left" in the general direction of his passive features, would our Kato quake and quiver?

No! He would simply fade back a step to evade the blow, or move his head slightly aside till the force of the blow is spent.

Then he would bring up both hands and firmly grab the

fighter's fist. He'd bend it backward toward his opponent's chest, stepping forward to do so.

He would then jerk the fighter's right arm to his own right side, causing the fighter to fall to the right and become somewhat off-balance, since his left foot would have been yanked off the ground.

Having him in this unbalanced position, little Kato would place his left foot behind the other's left foot (the only prop which now supports his body) and thereupon, by a backward kick of his heel trip that remaining leg from under him.

You finish the rest!

Where else would the fighter go—but down?

Look: (*See Fig.* 31)

Having witnessed an event as described, would you thereafter again put your money on a whisker and a scowl?

Now, if you are still unconvinced, or if by now your sympathies are entirely with the fighter—you having by this time discounted his pugilistic ability—and you think him the underdog, we will reconstruct another scene for you, with another and perhaps more apt boxer.

This one is less the "haunter-of-houses" and more the scientific type. He is a shadow-boxer of no mean talent. And he has dynamite in each fist, — if it lands.

He too leads with his left. He would be thrown out of the Boxer's Union if he did anything else.

Our Kato is prepared for that. He anticipated it.

He steps lightly to the left of that "left." The boxer, encountering good clean ozone, keeps moving forward, hoping to meet some solid body sometime.

Kato whirls until he is behind the boxer. He interposes his right leg between the boxer's two, and the point of that interposed foot bends inward until it hooks onto the fighter's left shin-bone, pulling him still further forward.

Then to finish it off, little Kato bends forward and brings the heel of his right hand directly into the back of the boxer's head, at the base of the skull, so smartly and with such force, that the premier of pugilism pitches forward on his face as though propelled from a cannon—his underpinning having been taken from under him by that skillful toe. (*See Fig. 32*)

May not our saffron-hued friend be pardoned for a slightly supercilious grin?

Let's not be superior? Can't we learn something from our diminutive oriental?

IN WHICH AN UNTUTORED RIGHT RECEIVES INSTRUCTION

If the student notes any lilt to our tone, he may get the idea we advocate Jiu-Jitsu as a panacea for all ills. Well there is one thing it positively will not do. It will not cure a stomach-ache.

But the south-paw (or, if our reader is not up on literature, the "lefty") who leads with his right, is a "sucker" for the curative value of Jiu-Jitsu. He can readily be relieved of all desire to use either right or left.

We have him, then, throwing that itching right hand toward you. If you know the "gentle art," you have medicine for this disease:

You just step back, resting heavily on your right foot.

Thereafter you bend your knees slightly, throw your right hand forward until it meets his right arm, with which he intended to strike you. You push it aside with your palm, but at the same time grab his wrist and jerk it forward and to the right.

He was going in that direction anyway, so he won't notice that he is going there a bit faster.

In the meantime you shift your own position so that you are to his right side, having swung him with you, although he is flying outward and away from you by centrifugal force.

You further help his progress by kicking your left leg in front of and into his right shin-bone, which must make that pin insecure to say the least.

Further to assist his departure you push his right elbow with your left hand, and then let go his right wrist.

Fig. 33

He will shoot forward into some outer darkness, like a falling star. (*See Fig.* 33)

MILL RACE (or Pin Wheel)

The Marquis of Queensberry, thinking only for gentlemen of his own caliber, developed a system of fighting—or as he then termed it, boxing,—which would make the then common brawl more palatable to the sporting gentry of his time.

We moderns have improved upon his rudimentary rules to such an extent, and have so widespread its knowledge, that to-day everyone knows something about boxing, and most of us in this country know enough about it to leave it to specialists.

Yet brawls, like the poor, we always have with us. And

Fig. 34

brawlers, with or without a knowledge of Queensberry rules, manage to avoid or forget any science when engaged in a heated physical argument.

Thus, if you are where, perhaps, you shouldn't have been at all, and you are involved in an argument with someone built on the grand plan, and object strenuously to his remarks, you had better forsake boxing rules and regulations and remember your Jiu-Jitsu.

For your intellectual giant will most likely sneak up behind you and throw his arms about you in a bear-like hug, which he believes will put you out of the race.

Fig. 35

Then, standing in front of him, with his gorilla arms squeezing you, what do you do? (*See Fig.* 34)

You bend quickly to your knees.

His arms which were around the upper part of your body, encircling your torso, will naturally slip higher, and your arms will be free of pressure.

You will reach up—grab his right wrist with your left hand, squeezing with all your might; grab his right hand with your right hand, so that your palm covers his hand and the fingers of your hand lap over into his palm.

Now, with a pull on that right arm with both your hands you will shift him to your right shoulder, and then—straightening up

Fig. 36

suddenly you will heave your right shoulder to the right, sending him flying over your right shoulder and onto his back on the floor in front of you.

Since you have not chosen the particular place where he must fall, it may be that he will have landed without much gentleness in such a spot as would be conducive to insensibility.

Should he, however, be one of those creatures whose head is more concrete than the floor and show signs of further combativeness, you merely drop on his body with one knee, making sure you land on his flattened shoulder and then press on his other arm with one or both of your hands. (*See Fig.* 35)

To a rough-and-tumble fighter you have illustrated the millrace or pin wheel, so vividly, that if he recovers, he will also have gathered a new respect for his fellow man and will ever after forego the pleasure of hugging his opponent lest he again be initiated into the mysteries of Jiu-Jitsu. (*See Fig.* 36)

MILL RACE (modified)

If you have carefully studied the previous chapter on the Mill Race, and its accompanying illustration, even before you have attempted to carry out its instructions, you may have asked yourself a very pertinent question.

You, professor, have very casually assumed that my opponent will be a brawler or cut-throat who knows nothing about the science of Jiu-Jitsu. What, pray, is to prevent my attacker from knowing a thing or two about it, and while he thus hugs me from behind and I bend to neatly throw him over my head, he should bring up his arms and obtain a strangle hold on my neck?

Well asked. It would be suicide to always go on the assumption that your opponent knows nothing. He may know something, even if he is in the place where you shouldn't have been. He might have the same reason for being there that you have.

All right. Let's reconstruct the crime.

You are standing in front of your "bear that walks like a man" and he has his arms about you, squeezing you mightily.

You have sunk to your knees. His arms loosed their hold and slipped higher and are now near your throat.

You give him credit for the same specialized knowledge you

have. You expect him to try to gain that strangle hold. What do you do?

You lift your left arm out of the loop formed by his arm around your neck, reach across that left arm of his, thus breaking his hold around your neck. You continue the motion. You place your hand around both of his legs which are in back of you, gripping them in back of his knees and drawing them together.

Fig. 37

Your right arm, which is still under the loop formed by his right arm over and around your neck, you raise until it is loosened from the pressure of his right arm; then you reach across that right arm, loosening that right arm from his grip around you, and continue on till you have seized the wrist of his left arm. He couldn't strangle you now or ever hereafter.

But you are not finished. He may be captive but still dangerous.

Now you rise from your knees, but remain slightly bent.

You swing around with his body to your left—heave your right shoulder to the right, urge his legs upward with your left arm, and releasing your holds simultaneously, you throw him over your head to the right. He will most assuredly land on his head or some other part of his body.

Fig. 38

From there on, you can repeat the previous lesson. Just drop your knee or knees, if you wish, on his body and hold him thus imprisoned. (*See Fig. 37*)

All of the foregoing, presupposes that you have learned this lesson by heart and so thoroughly digested it, that you can execute all of the holds and motions like an automaton. For it to be serviceable, it must have become second nature with you. You have no time for independent thought. Any slight pause may become fatal, particularly if your victim knows something about Jiu-Jitsu. (See Fig. 38)

BREAKING A HABIT

With the modern girl pretty nearly emancipated from all the taboos which in the past might have made her a lovely object to look upon but a singularly defenseless creature, who are we, mere man, to devote no space to her further education?

Assume that Miss Kate doesn't like one of her many suitors.

He's an obnoxious person. Her beauty arouses in him no protectice instinct. He doesn't believe that the beautiful charmer is entitled to any freedom. In fact, he's always trying to imprison her waist, if and when she ever permits him to come close enough to her.

Oh yes, she's remonstrated with him often enough, but his male ego makes him imagine the feminine "No" always means "yes." She is a lady and would like to break his head, but being a lady, she only wants to break him of the habit.

He stands, therefore, on this momentous occasion, to her left while his right arm attempts to steal around her waist. She doesn't resist him this time. He is more than astonished. This is his first success.

Suddenly she swings her left arm over that lawless right arm of his, until her forearm is around his arm right above his elbow.

She exerts a little pressure on his arm without moving her body, so that the man's arm becomes rigid. He can't even wriggle it.

Then she swings her left leg in back of her, steps forward with her right leg, until the heel of her right foot is directly in back of hero's right heel. He cannot retreat, if he would.

With her right hand finger stiffened, she slams the heel of her hand against that unfortunate suitor's chin, snapping it backward.

Willy, nilly, he moves backward. He stumbles over that right leg of hers.

She releases the captured arm and his own backward momentum topples him over on his back. (*See Fig.* 39)

She is now completely free of one more inhibition, and one "very bad hombre."

Fig. 39

Suffice it to say that we do not advocate the lady's going about wreaking havoc on all males in this manner. After all some of us do wait for an invitation.

THE PUSH OVER

By now our student should know enough about Jiu-Jitsu to stop him from being a "push-over" for almost any sort of tough customer.

But with the acquisition of this lesson, the "PUSH-OVER," he will begin to appreciate the really fine points of the science. Here we will no longer pit him against rank amateurs who are at a disadvantage because of their ignorance. We'll give him a worthy opponent.

Let's call in little Kato again. Remember, we do not say that our student will win the bout, but it will be worth while getting a lesson from a master.

Come, Mr. Student! Stand here to the right, and face Kato.

Fig. 40

We needn't ask Kato to do the same because he knows just what we are going to demonstrate.

He places himself facing you.

Now, then. Reach out with your right hand and grasp Kato's

left lapel, right near his left ear. Of course Kato will do the same thing to you.

Then grasp Kato's left arm under his left elbow. Kato knows. He's doing the same thing to you. Up to this point you are even. Neither of you has any advantage. But watch carefully. (*See Fig. 40*)

Kato is pushing you away from him. What else can you do but resist and attempt to push him back. He's even trying to place a foot in back of you, but you spread out both your feet so that he can't get that trip hold on you, and continue pushing him back.

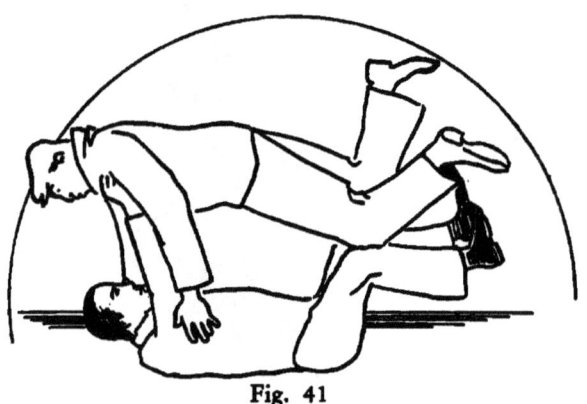

Fig. 41

He's resisting you, but he looks puny and as this tug of war goes on you are gaining over him. He's being pushed further and further back.

In fact Kato seems to be sagging. He's sitting down. Now you've got him. Or have you? Look out! That wily little fellow is as tricky as a bucking bronco.

Why, look! He isn't sitting, he's lying down and he's drawing you down with him. In fact you are on top of him.

Now you'll squash him like a nice, fat little grub-worm.

Horrors! What is he doing?

He's raising his feet. They are lifting yours above his body. He's kicking his feet upward and your feet are being thrown upward away from his body.

He's lifting your chest from his with his powerful little arms and heaving with all his might. His legs have risen higher. They are no longer resting against your legs. They are resting against your stomach.

He gives a mighty heave with his legs, releases his hands from your collar and elbow. And where are you?

Why, flying over his head!

Yes, you've landed. Everything that goes up must come down. But you are on your back.

Pshaw, don't make such a fuss about it. It didn't really hurt! You are not even bruised. Well, perhaps your pride is a bit hurt. Such a pitiful little fellow should do this to you.

But take comfort. Kato is a master. He could have done the same thing to a man much bigger than you. Now—go thou and do likewise.

Here's how it will look in a diagram: (*See Fig.* 41)

PUSH AROUND

Now that we have gotten Kato into the gym with us and had him demonstrate for us the "Push Over," much to the student's astonishment, amazement and little amusement, and yet having taken it all in good spirit, we must ask him further to instruct us in another variation of the "Push Over," for want of a better name for which, we will call it the "Push Around." This is much more descriptive than accurate a translation of the Japanese.

Kato is the best natured little fellow in the world. These is no malice to his gymnastics and he'd have no objection to your "doing him in" if you could.

Let's get down to business, however. This is no time for social amenities.

Place yourself in the same position as you did when you attempted that ill-fated "Push Over." That is, put out your right arm and with your right hand grasp Kato's right arm with your left arm at a point just above his elbow. He, in turn will grasp your right elbow with his left arm.

Now then, with your improved knowledge, both of you will begin see-sawing for a chance to grab some other hold, and so you won't push against him so hard as you did the last time. You are

Fig. 42

going to try not to repeat the same mistake twice.

However, Kato, is aware that you know something now, so he doesn't push you so much. He pulls you a bit. And when you are close to him, he tries something else.

He lets go your coat lapel with his right hand, and brings that hand inside your elbow, under it and places it against your chin on the left side.

Then rapidly he releases your elbow with his left hand, and draws his left arm over your right arm. Remember that you are holding his coat lapel. By drawing his arm over yours he compels your arm to remain rigid and in that position until he desires to change it.

He continues. He brings his left hand up further over your left arm until it touches his own right arm. Thereupon he grasps his own right wrist with his left hand. With this powerful leverage, he now pushes against your chin with might and main.

In the meantime, he has placed his right foot in back of your right foot, by having stepped forward with his right foot and then with the heel of his right foot he has interlocked his foot with yours, so that now that he is exerting pressure on your chin towards your left, since he is standing on your left side and has his leg in back of yours, you are bound to give way and fall backward over his prepared knee, or else find your neck snapped. (*See Fig.* 42)

This is hardly as strenuous a hold as the "Push Over" because it does not involve so elaborate a tableau. Yet, strangely, with less exertion, although with the same amount of speed and timing, the result is exactly the same.

This, of course, is the peculiarity of Jiu-Jitsu, that almost always the holds result in the victim being thrown to the ground. Usually this action drives all thoughts of further resistance from his mind.

It is a well-known fact that with loss of dignity comes a loss of the bellicose spirit.

However, should you desire to continue the feud, after you land on the floor, Kato's wiley eye would have seen it as soon as it occurred to you, and he would have sunk on his knee right on some part of your body, which act would have pinned you to the floor, unable to carry out your design.

TURNING TURTLE

Having enlisted Kato's assistance, we cannot very well show him that we are less polite than he. We know that nothing pleases him so much as letting him exhibit his prowess, and even if we must pay for it with a few bruises and sighs the following day, it will have been worth while.

Fig. 43

"Turning Turtle" he tells us is very like our old friend "Push Around," except in the manner in which the hold is obtained and in the manner of the "dumping" process. He says that what makes a turtle unable to move is to turn him on his back. Humans may have more intelligence, says Kato, but when they are dumped unceremoniously on their backs, they too find little to say (except some cuss-words) and some difficulty of locomotion.

"So," says Kato, "Stand in front of me just as you did when you were being shown the 'Push Around.'"

"I" says he, "will grab your arm, this left arm, right on the outside and in back of the elbow.

"Watch what else I do. I will hold on to your elbow, and then I am going to wheel, like this, and now I am in front of you, my back is against your chest.

"Still gripping your hand, I am going to bend forward like a jack-knife, but now it isn't necessary for me to keep holding your elbow with my right hand. Instead, I am going to release the elbow and grab your left wrist.

"When I bend you have to go with me. You are on my back, my right hand is holding tightly on to your left wrist.

"Suddenly I swing my body to the left, I pull your left hand to the right. I bend my body to the left, touching my left arm to the ground. My swing, the bending of my body must make you fall, but the pull of my right arm against your left wrist is going to turn your body in such a way that when you fall, you will sort of roll off my body to the ground on my left side, and you will naturally fall on your back." (*See Fig.* 43)

You will, of course, marvel that while Kato has been saying all this, he has been acting so quickly, that you could not even grasp the full meaning of his words when you found yourself on the ground.

I have, therefore, taken down his words here in this lesson for you, verbatim, so that if you study each sentence and phrase, you will begin to appreciate what it was he did to you.

Now try it on that long suffering friend of yours, that martyr to science who has helped you in every case but in those which Kato used you.

MUD TURTLE

Now that Kato has shown you a thing or two about "Turning Turtle" you can bolster up your ego by trying it out on your friend. But having done that you cannot stop. You are one of those incurable "correction and improvement" fellows.

While you are maneuvering about with your friend, you find

that he is a bit wary of your tricks. He has thus far suffered terribly from them, and he wants to protect himself against you, if he can. Well, you don't intend to let him do it, because you haven't found a bed of roses when Kato tried his stunts on you.

Your friend doesn't want to let you grasp his elbow, so you try something else. As you stand in front of him and attempt to grab his elbow, he brings his arm near you. You then grab his right wrist with your left hand.

Fig. 44

Having gotten that far, your friend is again in the toils.

You wheel around, holding on to his wrist, until you are in back of him, but in this case, your back is up against his back. You have pulled his arm across your left shoulder.

You bend down into a jack-knife again, so that now your friend is on top of you, back to back, but since you are holding on to his right wrist with your left hand and pulling his arm over your left shoulder, his body will shift to a somewhat left position.

Then you reach back with your right hand and grab his trouser leg in back of his knee, holding it firmly.

With a heave and a ho! you straighten up. His right arm you are pulling downward, his left leg you are holding rigid. By straightening up and heaving, you set him flying over your head and over your left shoulder by merely releasing both your hands from his wrist and trouser-leg. (*See Fig.* 44)

This time, however, since you have been holding him over your back and you have propelled him forward by the process of pull and heave, he will land not on his back, but most likely on his head, very much in the nature of a mud turtle burrowing into the mud.

THE SHEARS

Some of the "tricks" of Jiu-Jitsu are so ridiculously simple that one often wonders why no other nation ever thought of them before. Of course, the answer to that is, that no other race or country ever went in so scientifically to overcome a national handicap of small stature and centuries of ingrained culture and refinement.

For example, take the matter of the "Shears".

Now here is a hold that a child can practice. It is exactly the kind of a hold some youngster in terror of an older and more aggressive youth, would do well to resort to. Children like to grapple when in the throes of an argument. The resort to fisticuffs comes with age.

If your larger opponent grabs you by the shoulders, don't at first resist.

Come closer to him. Then bring your arms up inside of his.

Reach over with your right hand and grab his right lapel; then reach over and across your right hand with your left and grab the other's left lapel.

This, it can readily be seen forms a sort of shears.

Your wrists at this time are facing outward. You then press closer to him, and twist each one of your hands so that your wrists both face downward, each of them pulling the coat lapels tighter around his throat.

Fig. 45

If your pressure is strong enough, you would, if continued, choke or strangle your opponent into a state of complete insensibility, or if you do not desire such a grim end, you simply continue the pressure until you have choked the combativeness out of him.

To illustrate the action, look at the sketch: (*See Fig.* 45)

POLICE JIU-JITSU

The assumption throughout this lesson has been that the combatants are children. Surely what they can do, can easily be done by grown-ups.

With this knowledge, we are obeying for the benefit of the under-dog the biblical saying: "The first shall be last and the last shall be first."

FLYING PRAYER WHEEL

By now it must be the ambition of your life to turn the tables on Kato, if you are a red-blooded man.

Fig. 46

But you can't hope to do it unless you can be superior in guile to our tricky little Jap.

Suppose you ask him to show you that "Turning Turtle" again. He is a most gracious little man, and he immediately consents.

You assume the conventional pose. You stand to the left this time, and take hold of his coat collar with your left hand, and grip his left elbow with your right hand. He, of course, believing that he is going to give you another lesson, will hold your right lapel with his right hand and your left elbow with his right hand.

Suddenly you release his left lapel, turn your body to the right, throw your left arm over his left arm which you are still grasping with your right hand.

In the meantime you release his left elbow and with your right hand you grasp his left wrist, holding it close against your body and as rigidly as possible.

With the left arm you reach across his left arm, bending forward until your arm reaches between his two legs and grasps his left leg behind the knees.

Then you reach forward with your left leg and place it to the right of his right foot.

With a combined motion, you will heave his left leg upward, kick your left foot forward, tripping him, and with your right hand you will heave his left arm backward, so that all in all, he will fly to your left to land some distance away on his face. (*See Fig. 46*)

If it were any person but Kato, you would have no further trouble, because most people thrown thus violently would call it a day. But in this case, Kato will not take it amiss, if you follow up and whirl about, sinking your knee into his body on the ground, pinning him where he lies.

He is too much of a good sport to resent a skillful exhibition of Jiu-Jitsu, even if you have used the "Flying Prayer Wheel" on him to his own detriment. Life, Kato understands, is a question of give and take, and you can't always give it.

WHEREIN WE DISCUSS THIS AND THAT

Since our acquaintance with Kato Futsiaka, we have discovered that the little man is really a master of strategy, and that while he is small in body, his head has difficulty holding his mighty brain.

Of course, it is the Japanese art of getting at an object by indirection, that tinctures the whole philosophy of their lives and

Fig. 47

also affects the very physical things they do. Thus, their mode of attack is always by surprise.

Assume that Kato were to have a grudge against some one of those fullsome fellows that is always flowery in his praise when facing him but as nasty in his criticism once the object of his attacks is absent. Kato knows this, but his enemy doesn't know he knows it. Kato's idea is to make the fellow believe he is ignorant of his back-biting.

He meets him and as is the custom shake hands. The other,

Fig. 48

unaware of Kato's feelings, grips his hand in his **hypocritically unctuous** style.

Kato grips the other's hand. Steps back quickly, jerking the fellow's arm forward, and just as the other is about to lose his balance Kato bends downward, grabs the other's right leg at the ankle and then whirls his own body around, in such a way that his opponent is flying around on one leg (his left), his arm naturally trying to find a balance, and his right leg in the air, very much like some human windmill. (*See Fig. 47*)

Kato keeps whirling him around for a few moments and then releases both his right wrist and right leg, which promptly causes the other to fly out into space.

Kato turns calmly away, because he is indifferent as to where and when the other will land.

Kato, too, tells me he hasn't had such an easy time of it in school. His impeccable manners have set him off as a being apart. Where football is almost a religion, and rude individualism rules the roost, politeness can be a handicap.

However, says Kato, he has instilled respect in a number of these goal-post lifters. Intensely curious about American sports, he attended a football game. Being shy, he didn't exhibit the school's colors, and when his college won, he was swept with the mob onto the field and near the goal-posts.

For some unknown reason, a particularly heavy bruiser took him for a rooter of the defeated school. He grabbed our little Kato by the collar with his right hand. Then Kato exhibited the stuff he was made of.

When the bruiser held his collar and pushed him backward by placing his hand against Kato's chest, our little Jap did this: He brought up and thrust forward his left hand, grabbed the bruiser's right hand, pressing his thumb into that portion of his wrist back of the heel of his palm. Then he bent his own thumb and fingers so that the knuckles of these fingers pressed on both sides of the other's wrist.

He then pulled the other's hand close to his chest, thrust up his own right arm inside the other's outstretched arm and grabbed him by the coat collar, so that the bruiser couldn't move.

Thereupon he leaned forward, bending his knee so that his head came below the taller man's chin. Bending back the big fellow's wrist until the other groaned with pain. In an effort to break the hold the other threshed around with his free hand hoping to grab some portion of Kato's body.

Seeing the possibility of his hold weakening, Kato then straightened up and his hard head came in contact with the other's chin, with so much speed and force, that the other dropped backward to the ground as though he had been pole-axed.

Before the astonished spectators could recover their senses, one more college idol lay in a position reminiscent of the game they had just witnessed.

Of course, no other person interfered. Kato looked so calm and confident, so much the uncowed master, that not a few of them admired his cool courage, and some even asked him how it was done.

Kato has since gained a large measure of popularity. He is not averse to showing others how the simple holds and postures of Jiu-Jitsu may be tried with profit.

When asked to demonstrate it, Kato did, and then for the benefit of his new found friends, he made a sketch of the action. This is it: (*See Fig. 48*)

WRESTLING

Much as we admire the prowess of our Japanese friends, we must not in our zeal and enthusiasm, overlook the fact that while our American form of wrestling has to some extent borrowed a little from Jiu-Jitsu, our native product is far from something to be sneered at, and more than justifies its existence by the very great good it does as a body builder.

There is, of course, a great difference, in essence, between Jiu-Jitsu and our form of wrestling. Ours must of necessity be confined to the gymnasium. The grappling and the rolling, the grabbing and the attempts to release therefrom naturally cannot take place anywhere but on some canvas or mat, whereas Jiu-Jitsu by its simplicity and the fact that it is largely a defensive science, can be practiced anywhere.

POLICE JIU-JITSU

Nevertheless some of our holds bear comparison with that of the science of our Eastern neighbors, and in some instances are superior.

Just to give some idea how that may be, we are going to include in this volume a few of the simpler American Wrestling holds, and endeavor to show their purpose and usefulness.

We, too, are not without our pride.

BODY SCISSORS

One of the commonest and yet the most punishing of all holds in wrestling is the BODY SCISSORS. While, in itself, a simple and wholly understandable way of subduing an opponent, it, like

Fig. 49

most of the holds in wrestling, is only one in a pattern which must be woven together to obtain any given result.

In the sparring and jockeying for position—the seemingly useless pawing and groping, as it appears to the spectator—that opening which first reveals itself, is to the wrestler, the key to his campaign.

Assume that you are facing an opponent on the mat.

Somehow you have maneuvered it so that you are now behind him.

Fig. 50

Quickly you insert your left arm inside his left arm; under it and then over the back of his neck, until your whole forearm—the underside of it—is across the nape of his neck. Your fingers grasp the right side of his neck near his right ear.

You now have him pilloried so that he cannot move his head back, and unless he is a skilled wrestler, you may, by exerting pressure downward, snap his head forward and throw him to the mat.

Having this, what have you? Why, the HALF-NELSON, the most useful, yes, the almost indispensable hold of all. This is how it will look: (*See Fig. 49*)

But that is only a first step. You cannot really throw a good man by a simple half-nelson. He is a sturdy oak and must be brought down by something just a little more heroic. You must combine.

You proceed to try the BODY SCISSORS.

Holding tight to his neck, in that punishing HALF-NELSON, you use his body as a spring board. You jump up from the mat and throw both legs around his waist, so that the inside of your knees press against the sides of his body. Then you cross your legs at the ankles, gripping each foot with the instep of the other. Thus you have formed a giant pincer or scissors.

Your object, however, in wrestling is to pin his shoulder to the mat. If you have him there the required length of time, you will have won, or at least, be deemed to have obtained a "fall".

Both you and your opponent are still erect.

NOW, you throw your body backward to the mat, but manage it so that he does not fall on top of you, as if he does, his weight alone may pin you to the mat and prove your own undoing.

In falling, you twist to the left, retaining your HALF-NELSON and SCISSORS. Note the illustration: (*See Fig. 50*)

Having him on the mat, you continue the twining of your legs around his stomach, exerting your utmost pressure. This is bound to give him excruciating pain and shorten his wind.

The HALF-NELSON keeps his back to the ground and when the combined pressure proves more than he can bear, he will relax until his shoulder rests on the mat, and give up to superior force.

You will have won a fall.

No, not a gentle, nor even a gentlemanly pastime, perhaps, but clearly an edifying spectacle. Neither the victor nor the vanquished may smile serenely, as might a little Japanese wrestler, but to the winner it is nevertheless a highly satisfactory experience.

POLICE JIU-JITSU

TOE and ANKLE LEVER

As in Jiu-Jitsu, the objective is to secure such a hold on some portion of your opponent's anatomy as will make him realize the futility of further combat.

This is best accomplished, in wrestling, by picking the tenderest and most vulnerable section of the body, where a sudden twist or continued pressure would threaten eventual destruction

Fig. 51

of that member, or where the agony would be so great, as to create a desire for freedom even at the cost of defeat.

Such a hold is the TOE and ANKLE LEVER.

Given yourself and sparring partner.

Both of you have lowered yourselves to the mat, preparatory

to pouncing on each other. Naturally your backs are not on the ground touching the mat.

Suddenly you, on his right, slip your body—face downward—under his right leg. This will raise his body off the mat so that both of his legs are really on top of your body.

You will then twine your right arm under his right leg, continue on around until your hand rests on his left ankle above his heel. Now you straighten your body and get to your feet, still holding tightly to the imprisoned ankle.

It's clear to see that in standing you have lifted his body with you, or at least the lower part of his body.

Now you grab the toe of his left foot with your left hand. Your right hand under his right leg is still holding onto his left ankle. You proceed to bend and twist his ankle backward.

Your right hand acts as a vise to hold his ankle and leg rigid, while your left hand inflicts merciless punishment on his toe. Sooner than later, much sooner, for the pain is more than a human can stand, he will gladly give up the battle and sink to the mat on his back, signifying capitulation.

Simple? Watch the diagram. (*See Fig. 51*)

COMBINATION ARM and LEG TWINE and WRIST LOCK

Our form of wrestling differs from Jiu-Jitsu in one essential feature. The element of surprise is practically absent in wrestling.

Both gladiators are pitted against each other and prepared for any eventuality. It is largely a question of who gets there first. This offers more equality of opportunity and puts a premium on the possession of both brawn and brain.

The two sports or sciences illustrate, in essence, the very difference between the oriental and occidental mind and character.

To obtain a wrestling hold, as already indicated, it is often necessary to secure a few others, or to combine a number to produce one effect. This does not necessarily mean speed, but it very naturally demands presence of mind and a preconceived method of attack.

Again you and your friend are on the mat.

In the course of events he has managed to be on top of you and is attempting to secure some hold which would do him good and you as little as possible.

He is face to face with you and your mind clicks. This is the ideal position for the Arm and Leg Twine and Wrist Lock.

Then, let's go.

You wriggle your body to the right so that you shift him partly to your left and somewhat off your chest.

Your head is now to his left and to a degree this frees your left arm.

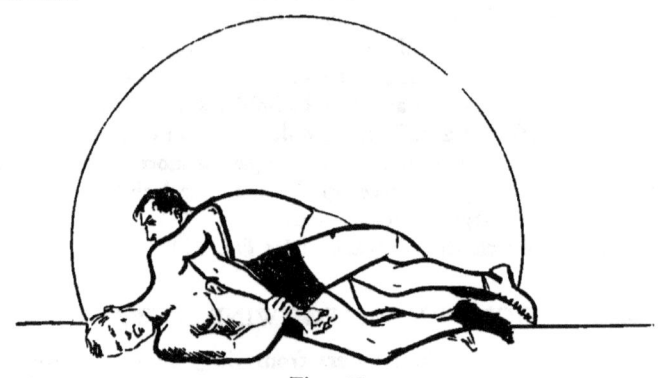

Fig. 52

Suddenly you seize his left wrist with your right hand and lock it tight.

Then you raise your left arm and throw it over his upper arm bending your elbows and twining your forearm around and under his biceps. Thus his left arm is wholly locked and encased as with steel.

Of course the rest of his body is free and you must remedy that—and soon.

You shift your body further to the right so that now your legs are free of his body and with a backward throw of your left

POLICE JIU-JITSU 87

leg, you twine the inside of your knee around the same part of his knee, like ivy around a stick or string.

Having him so, you need only roll over to your left, retaining your arm and leg twine and wrist lock. He must roll with you and your holds make him roll under you. You are now on top of him and all you have to do to complete his downfall is to turn face down on his body and the weight of your body coupled with the terrific pressures you are exerting on his captive limbs will cause him to relax to the mat, unable to stand the pain and the weight. (*See Fig.* 52)

THE STOCKS or CHANCERY and BODY CHECK

To those of a literary bent the word Stocks connotates a form of punishment meted out in old colonial days by our Puritan forefathers to those who would not conform, but in spite of the notoriously unliterary minds of our wrestlers, even the most cauliflowered knows the meaning of the word Chancery.

To have your head in Chancery is a most gruelling experience.

Fig. 53

88   POLICE JIU-JITSU

But whether you call it Stocks or Chancery, it merely means getting your arm around the back of an opponent's neck, so that the biceps of your arm rest on the nape and the forearm under his throat, and keeping his head imprisoned. (*See Fig. 53*)

Fig. 54

However, one well versed in wrestling tactics, might thresh his body around like some gigantic spider in the effort to dislodge this incubus that holds his head in Chancery, and the very whirling of his body and the freedom of his arms and legs might well break the hold.

Apparently the only thing to do is to use some additional means of stilling that heaving body.

Having obtained the Stocks or Chancery, therefore, the attacker, standing in front of the other and holding his head under the crook of his arm, reaches over with his free arm and inserts it under his opponent's arm and then draws it around the latter's body at the waist. Pressing on the nape of the neck and squeezing at the throat, and in addition, holding the waist rigid, makes the defender a complete prisoner. This might be called the BODY CHECK or BAR. (*See Fig.* 54)

It is a simple matter then to lower his body to the mat, where since he cannot release himself from the arm that is slowly strangling him, he will straighten out, knowing that his only out is in putting his shoulders to the mat.

ARM PULL and CROTCH LIFT

To our discerning student of Jiu-Jitsu the ARM PULL and CROTCH LIFT will present little mystery. He will easily recognize it even though our Japanese friends call it by another name.

The fact that it is popular with wrestlers the world over indicates how universal certain holds are and how effective, regardless of creed or color.

This hold is best used when the wrestlers are both standing.

Get your friend on the mat and follow the action, thus:

As you close in on your friend, bobbing and weaving in an effort to obtain some hold, you notice that for once, he is holding his arms down to his sides.

You grab his right arm at the wrist with your left hand.

You then bend at the waist and bring your shoulders up against his stomach, dragging his right arm across your left shoulder and holding it rigid.

Then you insert your right arm between his two outstretched legs and grasp his right leg above the inside of his knee and somewhat below his right buttock.

Now you straighten up, pull on his left arm, heave with your right shoulder, and suddenly release both holds, throwing him over your shoulder on to the mat. (*See Fig. 55*)

If this were Jiu-Jitsu, that would be the end of the action, because as indicated heretofore, the element of surprise would have played such a large part of the trick, that your opponent would hardly have recovered therefrom and most likely he would have landed on some hard object to his own imminent destruction.

Fig. 55

In wrestling, however, this sort of throw would only lead to some other hold, because the wrestler thrown would have fallen on a mat, and would be as agile as his opponent and would manage in some way to fall, if at all, on his hands or feet. You see, again, he would be prepared for any such eventuality and would, in his mind, have worked out a counter-action.

FLYING MARE

A variation of the ARM PULL and CROTCH LIFT is the FLYING MARE. It is easier to execute, simpler to understand, and is usually quite as effective and damaging.

In watching professional wrestlers, you will note the swelling biceps, the heavy necks and the gargantuan waists of the human elephants that grunt and groan for your entertainment. Aside

Fig. 56

from the show these pachyderms are putting on in order to impress the uninitiated, they use real science. And while you may get to think that they are a bit muscle bound, you will, if you are observant see that every muscle of their huge bodies is used in the action.

Suppose we try to analyze the Flying Mare which you will see more often at these professional matches, and place ourselves in the positions of the two "matters". Oh, we mean you and a partner.

You are standing in the middle of the mat, face to face.

Suddenly you seize his right wrist with your left hand.

Holding it, you whirl around so that your back rests against his chest. You pull his right arm over your right shoulder.

Then you reach around his arm, until your right arm grips his right biceps, holding the arm rigid.

Quickly you bend your body at the waist, pull forward with both your hands on his right arm, heave your right buttock into his stomach, like a bucking bronco, and with might and main heave him over your shoulder. (*See Fig. 56*)

IN WHICH WE DISCUSS WRESTLING GENERALLY

To say that we have illustrated even a tithe of the holds used in wrestling would be to insult the intelligence of the reader, who by the very fact that he seeks to teach himself through this medium, is of necessity a searcher for truth.

That, in these few chapters, has hardly been our object.

We have delved at length into the intricacies of Jiu-Jitsu, because we have felt that this science more nearly approximates what every normal and unbelligerent individual would like to know, as in the ordinary walks of life, it is seldom possible to place oneself in the position of a wrestler in the ring. If one steps on our toes, literally or figuratively, we cannot very well invite him to go to some gymnasium and have it out in a wrestling bout. There is neither the time nor the inclination to argue out the rights and wrongs of the situation. The attacker is usually one who is hardly amenable to reason and the heat of his anger leaves him no such thinking power as will lead him calmly to arrange for future combat, under rules established by gentlemen.

There is just time for a quick and sudden punishment. Therefore, the man who is prepared in himself to inflict it upon an opponent, with as little fuss and pother as the circumstances warrant, is the man of the hour. He can instil respect and gain for himself no little admiration by his quick thinking and trained prowess.

However, there does come opportunity to each of us at one time or another, when we are called upon to exhibit some knowledge of a primary sport known to almost every schoolboy. Wrestling on the beach, and in the gymnasium, whether for the purpose of impressing friends or in order to appear no such weakling as reluctance would seem to indicate, has become almost a part of the average American's extra-curricular habit. That being true, one must at least familiarize himself with elementary principles of wrestling.

Thus we have gone but lightly into a few of the holds in wrestling, trusting that even this small smattering of the knowledge will inculculate a desire to study the subject further and at length.

THE END

www.ingramcontent.com/pod-product-compliance
Lightning Source LLC
Chambersburg PA
CBHW071010160426
43193CB00012B/1989